PHONICS CHAPTER BOOK 16

THE GREAT TIME TRAVEL RIDE

by Robert and Anne O'Brien
Illustrated by Diane Paterson

Scholastic Inc.
New York   Toronto   London   Auckland   Sydney

No part of this publication may be reproduced in whole or in part, or stored in a retrieval system, or transmitted in any form or by any means, electronic, mechanical, photocopying, recording, or otherwise, without written permission of the publisher. For information regarding permission, write to Scholastic Inc., Instructional Publishing Group, 555 Broadway, New York, N. Y. 10012.

Copyright © 1998 by Scholastic Inc.
SCHOLASTIC, SCHOLASTIC PHONICS CHAPTER BOOKS, and associated logos and designs are trademarks and/or registered trademarks of Scholastic Inc.
All rights reserved. Published by Scholastic Inc.
Printed in the U.S.A.
ISBN 0-439-12328-3

1 2 3 4 5 6 7 8 9 10   23   08 07 06 05 04 03 02 01

Dear Teacher/Family Member,

Scholastic Phonics Chapter Books provide early readers with interesting stories in easy-to-manage chapters. The books in this series are controlled for sounds and common sight words. Once sounds and sight words have been introduced, they are repeated frequently to give children lots of reading practice and to build children's confidence. When children experience success in reading, they want to read more, and when they read more, they become better readers.

Phonics instruction teaches children the way words work and gives them the strategies they need to become fluent, independent readers. However, phonics can only be effective when reading is meaningful and children have the opportunity to read many different kinds of books. Scholastic Phonics Chapter Books cover many curricular areas and genres. They are carefully designed to help build good readers, but more importantly, to inspire children to love reading.

Contents

Chapter   **Page**

1. A Walk by the White House 4

2. Claude and the Statue 12

3. The Sprawling Bridge 18

4. The Tall Arch 24

 A Walk by the White House

A fair was in town. Bob and his friend Matt walked around the stalls. Bob played a game. He tossed three balls at a hoop, but he didn't get any in. Matt tried, too.

"Bob! Matt!" someone called.

"Look!" said Matt. "There's Mandy and Trisha."

"Hi!" said Trisha. "We're going to see all the new rides. Want to come?"

"Sure!" said Bob. "Let's go!"

"Rides make me dizzy," Matt said, walking slowly after them.

"Let's try this one!" Trisha called, pointing to a tall gray box that said "The Great Time Travel Ride."

"Wow!" said Bob. "Cool!"

A woman in the booth sold them each a ticket. "You have four tickets to four different places," she said. "Use them one after the other, not all at once."

"I'm not sure I like this," Matt groaned, as they stepped inside the tall gray box.

"I want to go first," said Trisha. She put her ticket in the slot in the wall and a paper slid out.

"It's a map!" cried Mandy. She read, "White House, 1829."

The tall gray box began to hum. The walls began to shake.

"We're falling!" cried Matt. Then the box stopped shaking. The door in the wall opened and the children stepped outside.

Once outside, they saw that the tall gray box looked different. It had turned into a horse and buggy.

Crowds of people were walking and talking to each other. All the women wore long gowns and all the men had on tall hats.

"Where are we?" asked Mandy.

A small girl stood there looking at them.

"Could you tell us who you are and where we are?" Trisha called to her.

"Why, I'm Ann, and you are at the President's house," she said. "You must know that!"

"And is it 1829?" Mandy asked.

"Why, yes, what a funny thing to ask."

7

"Well, we all have come from 19…" Bob started to say the year. But Trisha looked at him and didn't let him finish.

She quickly said, "We all have come from 19 Walter Street, in New York." Trisha didn't want Ann to find out about their time travel.

Mandy showed her friends a small map that said "White House, 1829."

"I think that's where we really are," said Matt.

"Wow," said Bob. "We sure did travel through time!"

"Why is everyone all dressed up?" Trisha asked Ann.

"Our new President said we could come to his house to meet him after he is sworn in," Ann said. "And tonight there will be a grand ball. People will meet in the great hall."

"Wow, cool," said Bob.

Ann looked at Bob. "Wow and cool. That's a funny way to talk," she said, not really understanding what Bob was trying to say.

"The White House is very beautiful," said Trisha, as she walked away with Ann.

"But it looks so different from the way it did when I saw it," Bob said. "Look at all the open space around it!"

"The White House is very beautiful now, but fifteen years ago, in the war, the British almost burned it down," said Ann. "I was not born yet, but my father told me how he and all the other men here used water to put out the fire. After the fire was out, workers had to rebuild the inside and the roof."

She pointed to a porch with tall posts. "That porch was just added on," she said.

Mandy looked at the map and said, "It says the posts in front are 40 feet tall." She took out her calculator. "Let's see. I'm four feet tall, so that's as tall as ten of me!"

Ann stared at Mandy. "Where are you children from?" Ann asked. "You are dressed in such a different way."

There were things that the children were not ready to talk about.

"Um, is that my mother calling?" said Trisha, walking quickly away. The others ran after her.

"Thank you!" they called to Ann, and jumped into the buggy. It was time to go to another place and time.

 # Claude and the Statue

Bob stuck his ticket in the automatic slot in the wall of the box. A map slid out. "Statue of Liberty, 1886," was written at the top. "That's in New York," said Mandy. "I know, because my grandpa lives there."

"And it says 1886—because that's the year we're go-go-going to," said Matt, as the box began to shake.

The shaking stopped. They opened the door and paused to look around.

"All the men are wearing hats," said Trisha. "And there are still no autos."

"See that woman and her little daughter—their skirts are so long," said Mandy.

"Look!" said Bob, after they stepped out. "Now the box has turned into a trolley. We're being hauled by a horse!"

A boy was selling newspapers on the street. A man tossed the boy two pennies. He caught them and threw the man a paper. The man caught it.

"Hello," Trisha called to the boy. "Which way is the Statue of Liberty?"

"Come this way," the boy said. They started walking. "I am Claude. You must have caught sight of the statue from the ship."

"Ship? What ship?" asked Bob.

"I know that you must have come by ship from a faraway place, because I have never seen outfits like yours," Claude said. "All the people from other lands come by ship. As they enter New York, the Statue of Liberty welcomes them."

"Well, we are from another place," Trisha began to say, thinking fast.

Just then they turned a corner and Claude paused. Then he called out, "There it is! Miss Liberty!"

"Wow!" said Bob. "It's all shiny!"

"It shines because it is made of copper," said Claude.

"But when I saw it, the copper had turned green," Bob said.

"Shhh, Bob!" said Matt. "Claude will find out about our time travel and it will be your fault."

"The statue was a present from France to America," said Claude. "It took ten years to build. In France workers made a big steel frame, then molded the copper into thin sheets. They hauled up the sheets and bolted them onto the frame. The statue is hollow inside, and you can walk up to the top and look out! It just opened this year."

"Americans gave money for building the base under the statue," Claude went on. "It took eight years to build, and wasn't ready until last August. I gave ten cents to help build it."

Mandy was reading the map. "It says that the Statue of Liberty is 305 feet tall. Since I'm four feet tall, that's…" She paused. When Claude wasn't looking she used her handy calculator and then shouted, "That's about 76 kids standing on top of each other!"

Claude looked up. "You are smart!" he said.

Matt spoke quickly. "You're smart, too, Claude," he said. "You've taught us a lot! But now we have to go." He added to the others, "Or we'll never get back!"

 # The Sprawling Bridge

They got back in the trolley.

"My turn," said Matt, yawning, "but I am a little tired. How long before we can go home?"

He put his ticket in the slot, and a new map came out. This one said, "Golden Gate Bridge, 1934." When the box stopped, they crawled out. They were on a hill on a green lawn. Behind them, they saw that the tall gray box was now a yellow cab.

"Where's the bridge?" asked Bob.

"It's just over this hill," said Mandy, drawing a line with her finger on the map.

"How long do you think the bridge is?" asked Trisha, as they walked.

"It's the longest bridge in the world, so far," someone said behind them. They turned and saw a kind-looking girl who had long black braids.

The girl had a small dog that had black paws. The black paws made the dog look as if he were wearing boots.

"Aw," said Mandy. "He's such a cute thing!" She shook the dog's paw.

"Hello," said the girl. "My name is May Lin. My dog's name is Paws. I see you are visitors. May I show you the bridge?"

At the top of the hill they saw the Golden Gate Bridge before them. It was sprawled across the bay.

"I'm glad that the bridge is there now," said May Lin. "Before we had the bridge, my father took a boat to work. He had to get up awfully early, just before dawn. I hardly saw him. Now there is time for us to read together each morning before he leaves for work."

"It says the bridge is 9,266 feet long," Mandy said. "That's almost two miles," she added, drawing her calculator out of her backpack.

Bob said to Matt, "Now I bet we'll hear how many times Mandy would fit on it. She loves big numbers." Matt yawned and patted Paws.

Mandy hid the calculator before May Lin could see it. "I can fit on there more than 2,316 times!"

Bob said, "There is one thing I want to know. Why is this bridge so great?"

"It's a new kind of bridge that's called a suspension bridge," May Lin said, sitting down to draw in the dirt. Paws sat down, too. "Before now, a bridge road was set upon big posts. Many posts had to be set in the water for a bridge to cross a wide space. In a suspension bridge, the bridge road hangs from big cords. Now bridges can cross wider spaces."

"Cool!" said Bob. May Lin gave him a funny look. "I mean, that is a good thing," he added quickly.

"Cool," May Lin said. "I like the sound of that." Paws wagged his tail.

Matt was still yawning. "I'm ready to crawl into bed. Time travel makes me awfully sleepy."

"Time travel? What is that?" asked May Lin. "I saw right away that you were not from here. But where are you from?"

Trisha said, "I think we have said too many things already. Let's go before it's too late."

"Bye!" they called. "Thanks!" They waved to May Lin and Paws, as they ran back to the yellow cab.

 The Tall Arch

"That was a close call," said Mandy. She put her ticket in the slot.

"Aw, I thought we were all done," said Matt. "Where are we going now?"

"Gateway Arch, 1965," read Mandy. The box shook and hummed again. This time, when they got out, the box looked like a bus. It looked very much like the buses from home.

"Look! Autos and airplanes! We are getting close to our time!" said Trisha.

They walked around on a lawn. Below a row of trees they could see a river.

"Where could the arch be?" asked Bob. "There is no one around to ask."

"Oh, no, now we are lost," moaned Matt. He turned around and said, "It's all your fault, Mandy." He paused, and looked up, up, up, as his jaw dropped. The others turned and saw a tall, silvery arch almost overhead.

"Wow," said Bob, "how tall is that?"

Mandy checked the map. She read, "630 feet tall." She hauled out her calculator one more time. "It would take 157 kids plus a bit more to be that tall. That is taller than two Statues of Liberty!"

"That's awesome!" said Trisha.

"Why did they put it here?" asked Mandy.

Trisha saw a boy walking by. She called to him, "Hello, can you tell us why this is here?"

The boy paused.

"It shows that we are proud of our city. It's the tallest arch in the United States!" he said.

The friends walked over to him.

Bob said, "Hi, I'm Bob. What's your name? And what is that?"

"My name is Paul," he said. "That is called the Gateway Arch. A long time ago, before this was the city of St. Louis, this was a place many people came before heading out West. Today the arch shows that St. Louis is still a good place to make a new start."

"Can people visit the top?" asked Mandy.

"Yes," said Paul. "There is a little car that goes all the way to the top. You can see all around for miles and miles. The people below you seem so small. They look like ants crawling on the ground."

"Can you walk around inside?" asked Bob.

"Well, it is hollow, but you can't walk around inside it," said Paul. "The only place you can walk around is the deck at the top."

"What is it made of?" asked Trisha.

Paul said, "It's made of stainless steel. That is why it can be so thin and still not fall over, even in a very strong wind."

"Thanks for the help," said Trisha. She turned to her friends. "We have to go back now because we have used all the tickets."

"All right!" said Matt. They all waved to Paul as they got on the bus.

As soon as they sat down, the walls of the box began to shake and hum. This time it did not feel like they were falling. It felt like they were going up—fast.

At last, there was a big thump, and the shaking stopped. Matt crawled out the door first.

"We're back already! We're at the fair!" shouted Matt. All the people in line waiting to get on the ride looked at Matt. The other friends crawled out, looking around them in awe.

"We really traveled back in time!" said Trisha.

"Yes," said Bob. "And the best part is, we traveled back home in time for dinner!"

Chapter Book 16: The Great Time Travel Ride

Vowel /ô/ a, all, au, aw

/ô/ a, all
- all
- almost
- already
- ball
- called
- fall
- falling
- hall
- small
- stalls

- talk
- talking
- tall
- walk
- walked
- walking
- wall
- walls
- Walter
- water

/ô/ au
- August
- automatic
- autos
- because
- caught
- Claude
- daughter
- fault
- hauled
- Paul
- paused
- taught

/ô/ aw
- aw
- awe
- awfully
- crawl
- crawling
- draw
- jaw

- lawn
- paw
- Paws
- saw
- sprawling
- yawning

Irregular Plurals

- children
- men

- mice
- people

- teeth
- women

r-Controlled Vowel /ôr/ or, ore, oor, our

- before
- born
- cords

- corner
- door
- four

- horse
- more
- porch

- wore
- York
- you're

- your
- yours

Words With /ə/ e, o

- another
- awesome
- calculator
- come
- different
- from

- front
- loves
- mother
- other
- others
- present

- someone
- the
- travel
- traveled
- welcomes

Homophones

- by
- bye
- for

- four
- hear
- here

- know
- no
- threw

- through
- to
- too

- two
- you're
- your